Isaac Asimov's

21st Century

Library of the
Universe

Past and Present

Exploring Outer Space

BY ISAAC ASIMOV
WITH REVISIONS AND UPDATING BY RICHARD HANTULA

Gareth Stevens Publishing
A WORLD ALMANAC EDUCATION GROUP COMPANY

Please visit our web site at: www.garethstevens.com
For a free color catalog describing Gareth Stevens Publishing's list of high-quality
books and multimedia programs, call 1-800-542-2595 (USA) or 1-800-387-3178 (Canada).
Gareth Stevens Publishing's fax: (414) 332-3567.

Library of Congress Cataloging-in-Publication Data available upon request from publisher.
Fax (414) 336-0157 for the attention of the Publishing Records Department.

ISBN 0-8368-3981-1 (lib. bdg.)

This edition first published in 2006 by
Gareth Stevens Publishing
A Member of the WRC Media Family of Companies
330 West Olive Street, Suite 100
Milwaukee, WI 53212 USA

Series editor: Mark J. Sachner
Art direction: Tammy West
Cover design: Melissa Valuch
Layout adaptation: Melissa Valuch and Jenni Gaylord
Picture research: Kathy Keller
Additional picture research: Diane Laska-Swanke
Artwork commissioning: Kathy Keller and Laurie Shock
Production director: Jessica Morris
Production coordinator: Robert Kraus

The editors at Gareth Stevens Publishing have selected science author Richard Hantula to bring
this classic series of young people's information books up to date. Richard Hantula has written
and edited books and articles on science and technology for more than two decades. He was
the senior U.S. editor for the *Macmillan Encyclopedia of Science.*

In addition to Hantula's contribution to this most recent edition, the editors would like to
acknowledge the participation of two noted science authors, Greg Walz-Chojnacki and
Francis Reddy, as contributors to earlier editions of this work.

Printed in the United States of America

1 2 3 4 5 6 7 8 9 09 08 07 06 05

Contents

• Exploring Outer Space •

We live in an enormously large place – the Universe. It's only natural that we would want to understand this place, so scientists and engineers have developed instruments and spacecraft that have told us far more about the Universe than we could possibly imagine.

We have seen planets up close, and spacecraft have even landed on some. We have learned about quasars and pulsars, supernovas and colliding galaxies, and black holes and dark matter. We have gathered amazing data about how the Universe may have come into being and how it may end. Nothing could be more astonishing.

One of the ways we have discovered the Universe is through the use of rockets. With rockets, we have been able to send probes to distant planets, and put artificial satellites into orbit around Earth, the Sun, and other bodies in the Solar System. We have sent astronauts into space, and some of them have even walked on the Moon. Rockets, probes, and satellites have contributed a great deal to unraveling the mystery of our vast Universe.

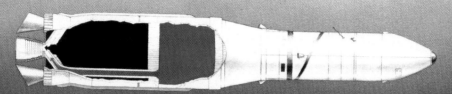

A rocket shows Newton's law of action and reaction. *(Upper)* Fuel, such as liquid hydrogen, and oxygen are sent to the combustion chamber, where they mix and ignite. *(Lower)* The hot gases created by the ignition rush out of the nozzle (the action), causing the rocket to move in the opposite direction (the reaction).

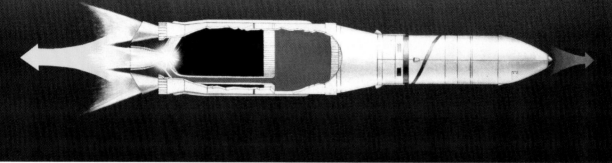

Right: As these three models from the seventeenth century show, rockets are basically tubes.

Below, left: The pieces of a seventeenth-century Chinese rocket arrow launcher are shown. Each hole in the launcher held a rocket, and all rockets could be fired at once.

Below, right: This is a drawing of an array of rockets used during the thirteenth century by Mongols in wars against nations and tribes in Japan, the Middle East, and Europe.

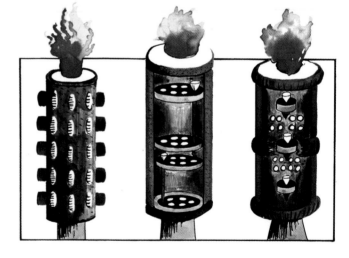

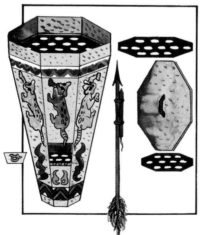

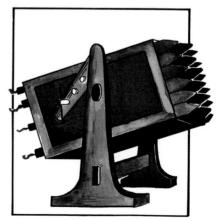

Rockets' Red Glare

The fascinating invention known as the rocket came about in a country that now has one of the world's largest space programs: China. In 2004, only Russia and the United States carried out more launches than China.

In China, people may have been using gunpowder to make fireworks as early as two thousand years ago. Sometime around the eleventh century, people started using bamboo or parchment tubes packed with gunpowder as weapons of war. When the gunpowder was lit by a fuse, gases were formed that pushed backward, moving the tube, or rocket, forward. In 1687, an English scientist, Isaac Newton, showed why the rocket moved forward when the gunpowder exploded. His explanation is known as the law of action and reaction.

In the early 1800s, Britain began using rockets to carry explosives in warfare. Francis Scott Key wrote about this in the national anthem of the United States, *The Star Spangled Banner*, with the words "the rockets' red glare."

Below: A rocket launches a Chinese communications satellite into orbit.

The Early Days of Rocketry

By the early twentieth century, some scientists had begun to realize that rockets were one way that objects could be sent into space. The first scientist to understand this was a Russian, Konstantin Eduardovich Tsiolkovsky, who published his ideas in 1903. An American, Robert H. Goddard, continued that work. In 1926, Goddard launched the first rocket using gasoline and liquid oxygen instead of gunpowder. For the next fifteen years, Goddard kept designing and launching better and better rockets. Unfortunately, rockets big and powerful enough to use in space also meant that some people would want to use them to carry weapons of war right here on Earth.

Left: In the early 1900s Konstantin Eduardovich Tsiolkovsky suggested ideas about rocketry that have since become a reality. His suggestions included using liquid oxygen and hydrogen to fuel high-speed rockets and using artificial satellites and rockets in space. Robert H. Goddard carried on this work.

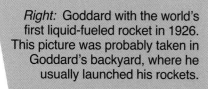

Right: Goddard with the world's first liquid-fueled rocket in 1926. This picture was probably taken in Goddard's backyard, where he usually launched his rockets.

Above: Goddard at Clark University in Worcester, Massachusetts, in 1924.

The ugly aftermath of the German bombing of London during World War II, when rockets were used.

Soviet cosmonaut Yuri Gagarin just before he took off aboard the spacecraft *Vostok 1* and became the first person in space.

The Space Age Begins

During World War II, the Germans developed rockets big enough and powerful enough to bomb London, England, and other enemy cities. After the war, both the United States and the former Soviet Union began to develop large rockets for exploring space.

On October 4, 1957, a Soviet rocket launched Earth's first artificial satellite. The satellite, *Sputnik 1*, weighed 184 pounds (83.6 kilograms), and it circled Earth in an egg-shaped orbit 142 to 588 miles (228 to 947 kilometers) high every ninety-six minutes.

A few months later, on January 31, 1958, the United States launched a satellite, *Explorer 1.* The Space Age had begun! Just three years later, on April 12, 1961, Soviet cosmonaut Yuri Gagarin became the first person in space.

Above: In the Russian language, *sputnik* means "traveling companion." On November 3, 1957, *Sputnik 2* became Earth's second artificial satellite. It carried a dog named Laika, the first animal in orbit.

Catch some satellite shine!

Some artificial satellites are visible from Earth. They look like bright stars moving slowly across the night sky. They can be seen best just after sunset or before dawn, when the satellite is already lit by daylight but the sky is still dark where you are. Artificial satellites are visible because they reflect light they receive from the Sun — just as Earth's natural satellite, the Moon, does.

9

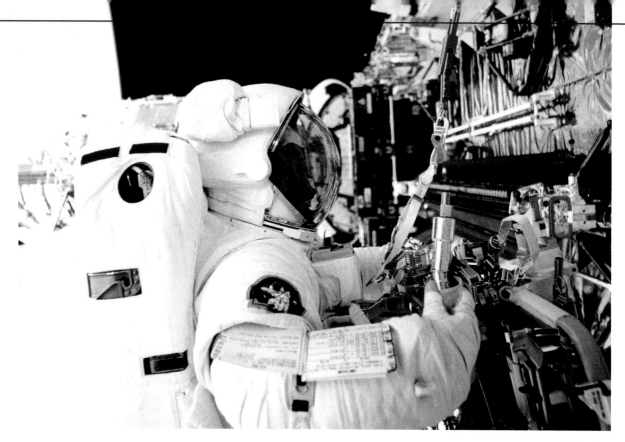

Above: In 1993, astronauts aboard the U.S. space shuttle *Endeavour* performed a series of demanding space walks to fix the Hubble Space Telescope. Here, astronaut Kathryn C. Thornton refers to a notebook on her arm to make repairs to the telescope.

Below: SpaceShipOne, the first privately developed craft to fly into space, is shown here attached to the bottom of its mother ship, the *White Knight*, which lifted it high in the air for launch.

Spacecraft That Can Be Reused

By the end of the twentieth century, rockets had carried many people and artificial satellites into space. But rockets can be costly. They can take a long time to make and are usually discarded after they are used. Some engineers think that vehicles that could be reused would provide a cheaper and more convenient way to travel into space. But such vehicles are difficult to develop.

In 1981 the United States launched the first of a series of partly reusable manned vehicles called space shuttles. These could carry heavy loads. Astronauts aboard the shuttles performed scientific research, launched satellites, and did repair work on satellites already in orbit. Unfortunately the space shuttles turned out to be very expensive to operate and suffered serious accidents.

Engineers hope to someday develop reusable "spaceplanes" that can take off and land on Earth like airplanes. In 2004 a simple reusable craft capable of rising just above the atmosphere and then landing made its first flights. Called *SpaceShipOne*, it was the first privately developed craft to fly into space.

Right: Most artificial satellites are launched by nonreusable vehicles, such as this huge Delta II rocket carrying aloft the *Spitzer Space Telescope* in 2003. The *Spitzer*, which orbits the Sun, detects infrared light.

Predicting Weather Conditions

The artificial satellites circling Earth do many kinds of work. Communications satellites send radio waves from one place to another that may be thousands of miles away. Thanks to them, TV programs and telephone calls can be sent easily from continent to continent. Navigation satellites give signals that make it possible for planes, ships, automobiles, or anyone with the right receiver, to pinpoint their location.

Weather, or meteorological, satellites are yet another example.

They take pictures of our planet, which they send back to Earth by radio. Such images – the source of the weather-related pictures shown on TV – reveal the movement of clouds. Observing this movement helps meteorologists predict the weather. This is especially important when dangerous weather is approaching. For example, before 1960, when the first successful weather satellite was launched, meteorologists couldn't always tell when a hurricane might strike.

Right: A dramatic image of Hurricane Ivan in September 2004, made by instruments on board NASA's *Aqua* Satellite

Below: Thunderclouds over the Amazon Basin, Brazil. The photograph was taken by the U.S. spacecraft *Apollo 9.*

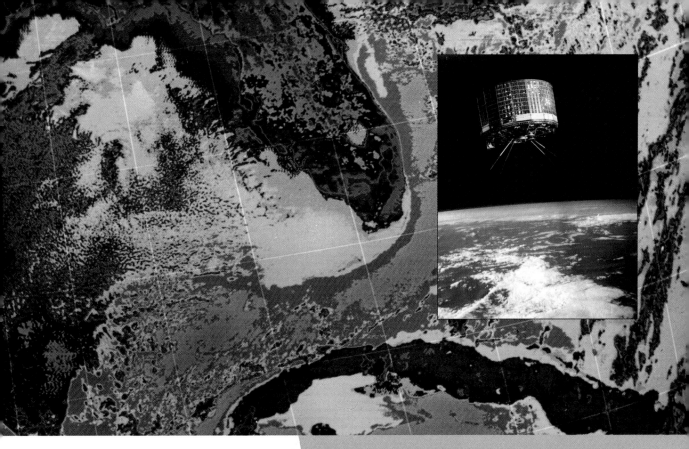

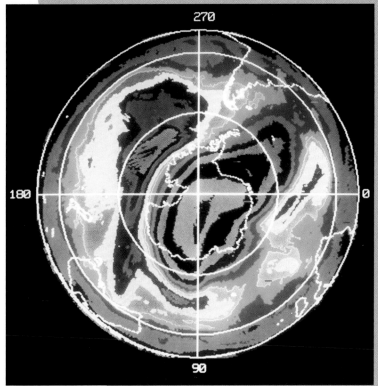

Above: A thermal (heat) map of Florida and Cuba taken by the weather satellite *Nimbus 5.* As indicated by the various colors, Cuba and the water along the Gulf Coast (in red) are warmer than Florida and Mexico's Yucatán Peninsula (in blue and green). In Florida, Lake Okeechobee (in yellow) and the Everglades (in red) are warmer than other parts of Florida.

Inset: Tiros 8 was a weather satellite sent into orbit in 1963 to take pictures of cloud patterns and instantly transmit them to Earth.

Right: A map containing information sent back to Earth by *Nimbus 7* shows the ozone layer that protects Earth from some of the Sun's ultraviolet rays. The dark violet area represents an area over Antarctica where the ozone is very thin. Scientists think this "hole" was created by chemicals released into the atmosphere by the modern world.

13

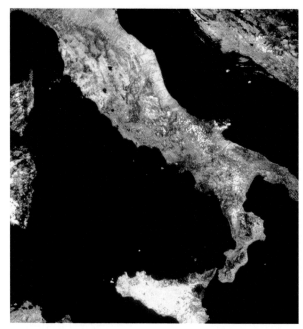

Above, left: High above Florida, the space shuttle *Challenger*, atop a plume of steam, heads toward outer space on its second mission, in 1983.

Above, right: Italy's "boot" is clearly visible in this satellite picture.

Right: A satellite view of the Arizona-Utah border area showing the Colorado River and the Grand Canyon.

Opposite: The eastern coast of the United States from New York City to Norfolk, Virginia, as seen by satellite.

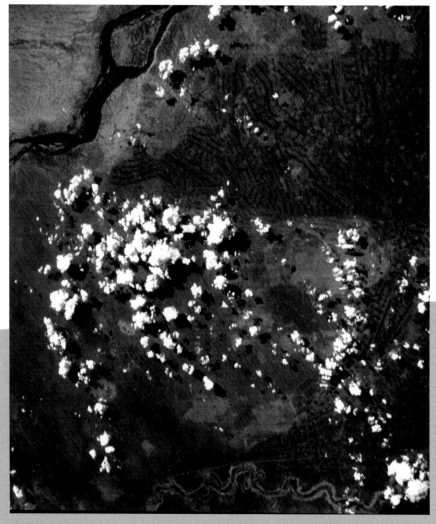

Studying Earth by Satellite

When clouds aren't in the way, satellites can take pictures of Earth itself. This makes it possible to have very exact maps of Earth.

Satellite pictures can also reveal the condition of forests and croplands, pinpointing trouble situations such as the spread of plant diseases. The ocean and its schools of fish can be studied by satellite.

Many satellites do this work from what is known as a geostationary orbit. They stay over one area of Earth at all times. In order to do this, a geostationary satellite must be about 22,200 miles (35,800 km) high. A satellite at this height can orbit at the same speed as Earth's rotation. This allows it to stay in one place above Earth. Geo-stationary satellites may be used for telecommunications, weather forecasting, and even spying.

Eyes in the sky, and ears too!

Spy satellites see amazingly well from orbit. Their exact capabilities are top secret, but as of the beginning of the twenty-first century, the best ones were believed to able to make out things as small as 3-5 inches (8-13 centimeters). Certain satellites can "see" using infrared light or radar — helpful when the view using ordinary light is blocked because it is too dark or clouds are in the way. And some satellites can eavesdrop on radio communications. Data from U.S. spy satellites are used not only for national defense purposes but also to assist relief efforts after major disasters, such as the tsunami in the Indian Ocean that killed nearly 300,000 people at the end of 2004.

15

Worlds Beyond

Artificial satellites orbiting Earth can tell us about other worlds, as well as our own. Some carry special telescopes that can peer far into the Universe by detecting visible light or other types of radiation, such as gamma rays, X rays, or infrared radiation.

Space probes can observe worlds in our Solar System up close. They even land on some of these worlds The nearest world beyond Earth is the Moon. It is about 238,900 miles (384,400 km) away. The first probe to reach the vicinity of the Moon was a Soviet craft, *Luna 1*, at the beginning of 1959. About nine months later another Soviet probe, *Luna 3*, raced past the Moon and returned pictures of its far side, the side that is always turned away from Earth. In July 1964 the U.S. spacecraft *Ranger 7* became the first probe to both hit the Moon and send back pictures. Five years later, a piloted spacecraft finally touched down on the Moon. U.S. astronaut Neil Armstrong became the first person to step onto another world.

Left: A view of the far side of the Moon.

Below, left: Apollo 11 commander Neil Armstrong in his lunar module on the Moon in July 1969.

Below, right: A view of the surface of the near side of the Moon from the spacecraft *Apollo 8*. The large crater is about 20 miles (32 km) across.

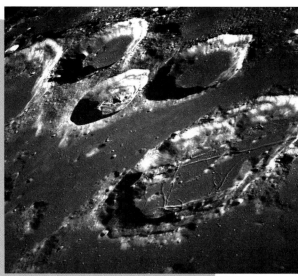

Above: An artist's rendition of an assortment of satellites and probes leaving home base, Earth, behind. *Clockwise, from upper right: Voyager* (U.S.), *Mariner 6* or *7* (U.S.), *Ulysses* (European Space Agency), *Pioneer* (U.S.), Hubble Space Telescope (U.S.), *Vega* (former Soviet Union), and *Galileo* (U.S.).

Right: In 1969, *Apollo 12* astronaut Pete Conrad poses with *Surveyor 3*, a robot lander that arrived on the Moon two and a half years earlier. Information from the *Surveyor* probes helped pave the way for human landings on the Moon.

17

Probing Mercury

No human being has yet gone farther than the Moon, but unpiloted probes have. In 1974 and 1975, a U.S. probe called *Mariner 10* skimmed by the planet Mercury three times. It came within 203 miles (327 km) of the surface, taking photographs as it went by. Mercury is the planet that is closest to the Sun. Before *Mariner 10*, Mercury was seen only as a tiny circle. The probe showed much of Mercury's surface in detail. It looks very much like our Moon, with many craters on its surface.

A fuller picture of Mercury is expected to be provided by the NASA spacecraft *Messenger*, launched in August 2004. The probe is scheduled to fly past Mercury three times in 2008-2009 and then go into orbit around the planet in 2011. The European Space Agency plans to send a mission called BepiColombo to Mercury in 2011-2012.

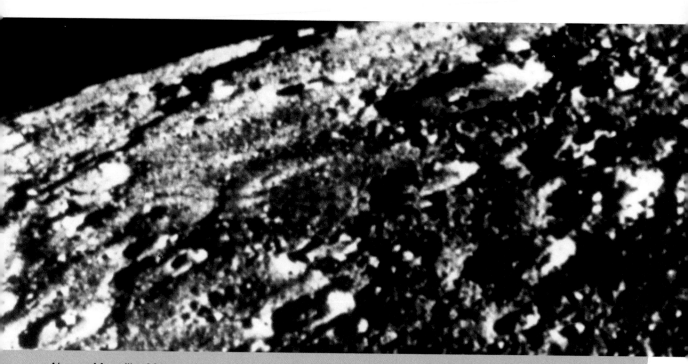

Above: Moonlike Mercury is the smallest of the rocky planets and the second smallest planet (after Pluto) in the Solar System. This photo was pieced together from many images taken by *Mariner 10* from a distance of 124,000 miles (200,000 km) above the planet.

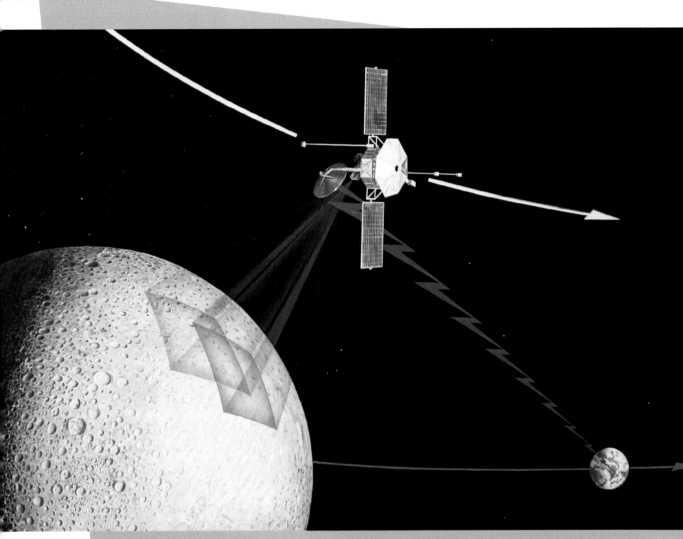

Above: This image illustrates *Mariner 10* swooping past the sunlit side of Mercury and transmitting pictures back to Earth.

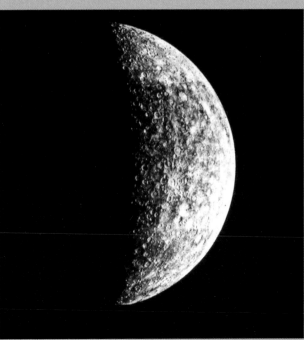

Right: With virtually no atmosphere to burn up metoroids and asteroids that hit it, tiny Mercury has taken quite a beating in its billions of years in the Solar System.

Unveiling Venus

Venus was first visited by space probes in 1962. Early probes showed that its dense atmosphere held in heat, making Venus even hotter than sun-baked Mercury. They also showed that the surface of Venus was always hidden beneath thick clouds. Landers sent back pictures of the surface before being destroyed by the intense heat.

Since radio waves can penetrate clouds, the first crude maps of Venus were made by radio telescopes on Earth. In the 1970s and 1980s, radar-equipped probes from the U.S. and the former Soviet Union orbited Venus and provided even better maps. The U.S. probe *Magellan* supplied the clearest pictures of Venus. It mapped 98 percent of the planet's surface by radar from 1990 to 1994.

The European Space Agency planned to launch a probe in late 2005, called *Venus Express*, that would go into orbit around the planet. NASA's spacecraft *Messenger* was scheduled to fly by Venus twice, in 2006 and 2007, on its way to study Mercury.

Probing the Venusian cloud cover

Venus is almost the same size as Earth, but it is closer to the Sun. Clouds covering its surface contain water and sulfuric acid. It was once thought that there might be life on Venus. However, probes have shown that the planet is extremely hot and, as a result, dry. Venus turns very slowly, making only one turn in 243 days. It turns in a different direction from most planets. Earth and almost all the other worlds in the Solar System turn from west to east. Venus turns from east to west.

A computer-generated view of Venus's surface, based on radar data. Maat Mons, a volcano 3 miles (5 km) high, looms in the distance. Bright areas trace ancient lava flows. Some of the flows partially cover the crater Melba, which is 14 miles (23 km) across.

Is There Life on Mars?

Could there be life on Mars? It's an old question. During the late 1800s and early 1900s some astronomers thought they saw thin, straight lines, called canals, on the surface of Mars. They thought intelligent beings might exist there. Photographs taken by a series of Mars probes, beginning in 1965, showed no signs of canals. The probes – including successful landers in 1976, 1997, and 2004 – did find canyons, dead volcanoes, numerous craters, and a thin atmosphere. They also found evidence that there once had been a lot of water on the planet's surface. Water is necessary for life as we know it to exist, but as of 2004, no solid evidence for the existence of life had yet turned up.

Right: A false-color map of Mars based on data from the orbiting *Mars Odyssey* spacecraft. The dark blue and violet areas show where the frozen soil contains higher amounts of hydrogen – possible evidence of the presence of water (in the form of ice).

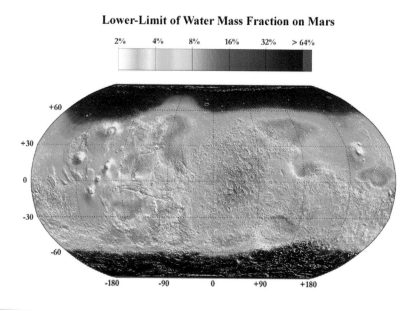

Lower-Limit of Water Mass Fraction on Mars

| 2% | 4% | 8% | 16% | 32% | > 64% |

Probing Mars – many questions remain

There are no canals on Mars, but there are markings on its surface that look like dried-up rivers. Probes orbiting the planet, as well as landers on the surface, have found much evidence that Mars once had abundant water. A little of that water appears to remain, in frozen form, on the surface, and some probably lies hidden underground, but what happened to the rest of it? During the time when Mars had a lot of water, did life develop? If so, are there any traces of life left today? Mars is the planet most like Earth, and anything we can do to answer these questions might help us better understand our own planet.

Above: The rover *Spirit*, one of two that began to explore the surface of Mars in 2004.
Inset: A close-up of a Martian rock studied by the rover *Spirit*. The hole and light-colored circles were made by *Spirit's* tools.

Right: A model of the two *Viking* landers, which began exploring the Martian surface in 1976. Each *Viking* lander weighed about 1,300 pounds (600 kg). Special features included a soil sampler (visible here extended in front) and two camera "eyes" sticking up just behind the sampler.

Journeying to Jupiter and Beyond

Four early U.S. probes – *Pioneer 10* and *11* and *Voyager 1* and *2* – are traveling on courses taking them out of our Solar System. But first, beginning with *Pioneer 10* in 1973, they explored the giant planets that circle the Sun at great distances. All four skimmed by Jupiter, the largest, and studied its natural satellites, or moons. They found live volcanoes on one moon, Io, and worldwide ice on another moon, Europa.

Beyond Jupiter, Pioneer *11* and *Voyager 1* and *2* also sent back close-up pictures of Saturn and its enormous rings. *Voyager 2* explored Uranus and Neptune as well. In 1989 it discovered rings around Neptune and ice volcanoes on the planet's moon Triton.

Above: Voyager 1 took this spectacular picture of Io, one of Jupiter's large moons. A huge volcanic explosion appears just over Io's horizon.

Probing Jupiter, a giant among giants

Jupiter is the largest of the planets. It is 318 times as massive as Earth. It has more than twice the mass of all the other planets put together. It also has many natural satellites, or moons. Four are quite large. One moon, Ganymede, is the largest of all the moons in the Solar System. In fact, it is actually larger than the planet Mercury! Jupiter's next largest satellite is Callisto. Both Callisto and Ganymede are made up largely of ice and are covered with craters. Jupiter also has a faint rings around it that were first discovered by probes, but they are tiny compared to the enormous rings of Saturn.

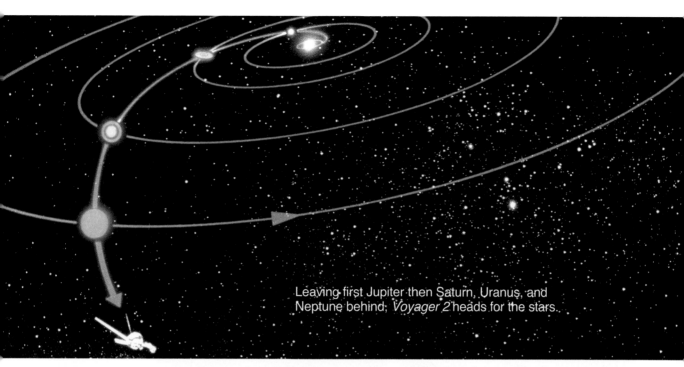

Leaving first Jupiter then Saturn, Uranus, and Neptune behind, *Voyager 2* heads for the stars.

Above: This picture made by NASA's *Galileo* craft clearly shows the flat, solid-ice surface of Europa, a moon of Jupiter. This view also shows the effect created by the interplay of the ice and colors on Europa's surface.

Above, right: An audio recording was carried aboard the two *Voyager* probes. Its material is geared to any extraterrestrials who care to listen and includes music and a greeting from former U.S. President Jimmy Carter.

Right: Voyager 2 photographed Saturn and its magnificent rings from a distance of about 2.1 million miles (3.4 million km) away.

Above: Saturn's rings as photographed by the spacecraft Cassini from a distance of about 4 million miles (6.4 million km).

Left: A false-color view of Saturn's giant moon Titan combining infrared and visible-light images made by the spacecraft Cassini in a close flyby in April 2005.

New Visits to the Giants

Before the end of the twentieth century, NASA sent two more spacecraft to the Solar System's two biggest planets. *Galileo*, launched in 1989 by the space shuttle *Atlantis*, was given the job of exploring Jupiter. *Cassini*, launched in 1997 from Cape Canaveral, Florida, by rocket, was assigned Saturn. While traveling to their destinations, both craft made valuable observations of bodies they passed along the way.

Galileo reached the vicinity of Jupiter in 1995. It released a probe into the giant planet's atmosphere. Before it was destroyed by high heat and pressure, the probe reported valuable information about conditions there. *Galileo* continued to explore Jupiter and some of its moons for several years. It burned up in Jupiter's atmosphere in 2003.

Cassini arrived near Saturn in 2004. It was expected to orbit the planet for a few years, studying Saturn, its rings, and some moons. Along with various instruments, the spacecraft carried a probe called *Huygens*, built by the European Space Agency. In January 2005, *Huygens* landed on Saturn's huge, moon Titan and sent back not only data but also fascinating pictures that gave scientists their first look at the moon's surface.

Discovering Saturn's moon, Titan

Until the *Cassini-Huygens* mission, very little was known about Saturn's largest moon, Titan, because its surface is blocked from view by a very thick smog-like atmosphere. In January 2005, *Huygens* dropped down through Titan's orange-brown atmosphere and landed on the surface — the first landing ever made by a spacecraft on a moon in the outer Solar System. Pictures of the surface sent by the probe showed channels that may have been formed by flowing liquid methane — it's too cold on Titan for liquid water. Radar observations made by *Cassini* showed other features as well, such as a huge crater about 270 miles (440 km) wide.

Fact File: A Sky Filled with Satellites

The nations of Earth have launched an incredible assortment of artificial satellites into space. These satellites give us new ways of understanding our Earth and outer space, predicting the weather, communicating with one another, performing technological experiments, and even spying on one another.

Although dozens of countries have launched satellites into space, only a few of these nations have their own launch sites. Therefore, many countries must use the launch pads of other countries. Some of the more important launch sites are the Kennedy Space Center at Cape Canaveral, Florida, and Vandenburg Air Force Base, California, in the U.S.; the European Space Agency's facility at Kourou, French Guiana; the Russian-operated Baikonur Cosmodrome in Kazakhstan; China's Satellite Launch Center at Jiuquan; India's Sriharikota Launching Range in the Bay of Bengal; and Japan's Kagoshima Space Center and Tanegashima Space Center. Some commercial satellites are placed in orbit by the private company Sea Launch (formed by four companies from the U.S., Russia, Norway, and Ukraine) from a floating launch platform in the Pacific Ocean.

Space stations – large satellites where people live and work for long periods – may someday provide a base for sending spacecraft to other parts of the Solar System. Early space stations such as the U.S. *Spacelab* and the Russian *Mir* were relatively small and were used mainly for scientific research. Assembly of a much larger *International Space Station* began in 1998. It is a joint project of the United States, Russia, Japan, the European Space Agency, and Canada.

Top: An artist's conception of a truly magnificent "satellite" – a space station hovering over Earth. The day will come when space stations will give us an ideal base for observing the cosmos and for sending probes and people to other parts of the Solar System.

Right: An artist's conception of the *Spitzer Space Telescope*, an artificial satellite that circles the Sun in an orbit trailing Earth.

28

Space Station Basics

Station: *Salyut*
Series of small stations — mass, about 40,000-43,000 pounds (18,000-19,000 kg) — launched by the former Soviet Union 1971-1982; *Salyut 7*, the last one, left orbit in 1991.

Station: *Skylab*
U.S. station — mass, 170,000 pounds (77,000 kg) — in orbit 1973-1979; manned 1973-1974.

Station: *Mir*
Station launched by the former Soviet Union in 1986; deorbited in 2001; mass, about 240,000 pounds (109,000 kg).

Station: *International Space Station*
Joint project of United States, Russia, Japan, European Space Agency, and Canada; assembly began in 1998; manned by crew since 2000; mass as of 2004, about 404,000 pounds (183,000 kg).

More Books about Exploring Outer Space

Artificial Satellites. Ray Spangenburg and Kit Moser (Franklin Watts)
Communications Satellites. Ann Byers (Rosen)
Earth Imaging Satellites. Jan Goldberg (Rosen)
The History of Rockets. Ron Miller (Franklin Watts)
Space Stations. James Barter (Lucent)
Spy Satellites. Paul Kupperberg (Rosen)
Weather Observation Satellites. Allan B. Cobb (Rosen)

DVDs

Inside the Space Station. (Artisan)
NASA 50 Years. (Madacy)
Welcome to Mars. (WGHB)

Web Sites

The Internet sites listed here can help you learn more more information about the development of rocketry and space exploration.

Encyclopedia Astronautica. www.astronautix.com/
European Space Agency. www.esa.int/esaCP
NASA. www.nasa.gov/missions/highlights/
Russian Space Web. www.russianspaceweb.com/
Solar Views, History of Space Exploration. www.solarviews.com/eng/history.htm

Places to Visit

Here are some museums and centers where you can find exhibits about rocket technology and space exploration.

Canada Science and Technology Museum
1867 St Laurent Blvd
Ottawa, Ontario K1G 5A3
Canada

Kansas Cosmosphere and Space Center
1100 N. Plum
Hutchinson, Kansas 67501

National Air and Space Museum
Smithsonian Institution
6th and Independence Avenue SW
Washington, DC 20560

New Mexico Museum of Space History
Highway 2001
Alamogordo, New Mexico 88311

Space Center Houston
1601 NASA Road 1
Houston, Texas 77058

U.S. Space and Rocket Center
One Tranquility Base
Huntsville, Alabama 35805

Glossary

Apollo: The U.S. space program that landed astronauts on the Moon several times between 1969 and 1972.

astronaut: a person who travels beyond the atmosphere of Earth. Russian astronauts are commonly known as cosmonauts.

atmosphere: the gases that surround a planet, star, or moon.

communications satellite: a satellite that receives radio waves from one location and then sends them to another, which may be thousands of miles away.

European Space Agency: an organization founded in 1975, pooling the resources of several European countries, for joint research and exploration of space. Canada is an associate member.

Explorer 1: the first U.S. artificial satellite, launched on January 31, 1958.

geostationary satellite: a satellite that is in orbit above Earth at an altitude of about 22,200 miles (35,800 km) and moves at a speed matching Earth's rotation. A geostationary satellite can stay over one area of Earth continuously.

meteorologist: a person who studies the weather. Some meteorologists specialize in weather forecasting.

methane: a substance composed of carbon and hydrogen that usually occurs as a gas on Earth but may occur in liquid form in very cold conditions, as on Saturn's moon Titan.

NASA: the space agency in the United States — the National Aeronautics and Space Administration.

navigation satellite: a satellite that gives signals that make it possible for planes, ships, and other vehicles having the right receiver to pinpoint their location.

orbit: the path that one celestial object follows as it circles, or revolves around, another.

Pioneer 10 and 11 and *Voyager 1 and 2:* probe traveling into the farthest reaches of our Solar System.

planet: a large celestial body that revolves around our Sun or some other star and that is not itself a star.

probe: a craft that travels in space, photographing and studying celestial bodies and in some cases even landing on them.

rocket: a vehicle used to launch satellites, probes, and other craft into space. A rocket carries its own fuel and oxygen for burning, and it is driven forward by hot gases escaping from the rear.

satellite: a smaller body that orbits a larger body. *Sputnik 1* and *2* were Earth's first artificial satellites. The Moon is Earth's natural satellite.

Solar System: the Sun with the planets and all the other bodies, such as asteroids and comets, that orbit it.

space shuttle: a mostly reusable U.S. space craft launched into space by a rocket but capable of returning to Earth under its own power. The first space shuttle, *Columbia*, was launched in 1981.

space station: a large artificial satellite in which people live and work for long periods of time.

Sputnik 1: Earth's first artificial satellite, launched by the former Soviet Union on October 4, 1957.

weather satellite: a satellite that produces pictures of occurrences such as cloud movements, which can help meteorologists predict the weather.

Index

Born in 1920, Isaac Asimov came to the United States as a young boy from his native Russia. As a young man, he was a student of biochemistry. In time, he became one of the most productive writers the world has ever known. His books cover a spectrum of topics, including science, history, language theory, fantasy, and science fiction. His brilliant imagination gained him the respect and admiration of adults and children alike. Sadly, Isaac Asimov died shortly after the publication of the first edition of *Isaac Asimov's Library of the Universe*.

The publishers wish to thank the following for permission to reproduce copyright material: front cover, 3, 23 (upper, both), NASA/JPL/Cornell; 4 (upper), © Sally Bensusen 1987; 4 (lower), © Laurie Shock 1988; 5, Xin Hua News Agency; 6 (left), Oberg Archives; 6 (right), 10 (upper), 11, 12 (both), 13 (all), 14 (upper left and lower), 15, 16 (all), 17 (lower), 18, 19 (both), 23 (lower), 24, 25 (center, right and lower), NASA; 7, 9, Smithsonian Institution; 8 (large), Imperial War Museum; 8 (inset), © AFP/Getty Images; 10 (lower), Courtesy of Scaled Composites, LLC; 12 (left), 14 (upper right), European Space Agency; 17 (upper), © Lynette Cook/Morrison Planetarium 1987; 20-21, Jet Propulsion Laboratory; 22, NASA/JPL/Los Alamos Laboratory; 25 (upper), © Julian Baum 1987; 25 (center, left), 29 (lower), NASA/JPL-Caltech; 26 (both), NASA/JPL/Space Science Institute; 29 (upper), NASA/Johnson Space Center.